REFUSE
TO LOSE

6 Ways to Overcome Obstacles
& Win the Game of Life

Odell A. Bizzell II

ISBN-13: 978-1523828104

ISBN-10: 1523828102

Contents

INTRODUCTION

The Game of Life

William Shakespeare famously wrote, *"All the world's a stage, and all the men and women merely players."* I say, life is a game that we all have to play and those that don't compete will never win. Whether you are a sports minded person or not, you have to play the game of life. Furthermore, keep in mind that everyone is always in a battle with an opposing force. Good is always in a battle with evil. Light is always in a battle with darkness. Health is always in a battle with sickness. Knowing this we would be wise to swiftly identify who our greatest opposition is.

Additionally why must you be competitive in the game of life? What does competition have to do with winning the game of life at all? How is all of this connected to you achieving your dreams and goals?

Here's a hidden truth you need to internalize; **the only person you should compete with is yourself**. The ultimate competition is the one you have within and you can only win the game of life by consistently competing to become a better you. The greatest battle we will ever have is with ourselves. On a daily basis we battle with what we expect of ourselves and what we actually experience. We also battle with following the path of least resistance or finding our own path to ultimate success. Every day we look in the mirror at our greatest opponent, yet most of us never acknowledge the enormity of the battle.

Just like Shakespeare's legendary words stated, all men and women are merely players, we are all players in this game called life. Unlike a competitive sports game, the only way to keep track of wins and losses in life is to measure the impact you have on others. This is what this book is all about, helping you win the game of life through making an impact on others. Winning is not about how much money you make or what you will make in the future, but winning can help you earn more money. Winning is not about how large your home is or how swanky your car is, but winning could potentially allow you to live in a nice house and drive a nice car. Winning the game of life can only be won if you create a life in which you positively impact everyone around you. Everyone that interacts with you on your job, in your business, in your service organization, at the gym, or at your school should leave that interaction a more valuable person

Throughout this book, the stories, illustrations, and principles shared will help you develop impeccable leadership skills, mental resolve, and above all the ability to impact others. Let this book be a part of the awakening necessary for you to live the type of life that leaves an enriching legacy that will last.

Before we start to discuss the 6 ways to win the game of life, I need you to identify the areas of your game you want to focus on strengthening. For example, in the game of basketball, the point guard usually has the responsibility to bring the basketball up the floor. It would behoove the point guard to learn how to dribble very well to help his team win the game.

One should carry this kind of focus into his or her life. People often lack focus on the few things that will make the most difference. If the point guard was focusing on becoming the best rebounder, jumper, and shot blocker, he would ultimately hurt the team by his lack of focus on his most important skills such as dribbling and passing.

So as you read this book, I want to submit to you that there are 4 areas of life that everyone needs to win in. These areas are: Faith, Family, Fitness, & Finances. No matter who you are, I recommend that you become positively obsessed with these 4 areas of life. Develop a sense of urgency about moving forward in all of these areas for as long as you live. Refuse to lose in these areas of your life.

When I go across the country speaking to students at high schools, universities, and small businesses these are the areas I help them win in. What's interesting is these areas in life are interconnected. Each one feeds the other in some form or fashion. The *Refuse to Lose* game plan you are about to learn is not about perfection in your performance, it's about progression within a positive obsession.

There's one thing I ask of you when reading and applying what you read: **Be tenacious, relentless, and consistent in your effort to win**. If you are a student just starting college, acknowledge that you will have to work hard to achieve exemplary grades. Recognize that you will have to get involved on campus to solidify a great future for yourself. If you are an entrepreneur that is just starting out in your business, this game plan will help you through the tough times all new businesses will experience.

Whether you are an executive of a corporation that leads hundreds of employees or a mom that leads 3 kids in the home, you can benefit from the information written in this book. Anyone that is at any stage in their life will be able to utilize these strategies to overcome the battles and wars they will face to win the game of life.

Though no one ever leaves this particular game alive, we can play it in such a way that more people win because of the legacy we leave.

**Losers quit when they fail.
Winners fail until they succeed.**

CHAPTER 1
The Refuse to Lose Game Plan

Sports has always had a huge influence on my life. I started falling in love with the sport of basketball in 1994 when I was 9 years old. My dad and I were watching the NCAA national championship game in which Duke and the University of Arkansas were matched up. I lived in North Carolina where Duke is located and was born in Arkansas so it was pretty cool to see those teams play. After Arkansas pulled off the victory, I was hooked.

After the final buzzer sounded, I turned to my dad and said, "I want to play basketball!" I then went to the park across the street and began putting up jump shots and practicing. I ended up being an above average high school basketball player, but I wasn't good enough to play major college basketball like I wanted to. I was however able to attend North Carolina State University where I worked for legendary women's basketball coach Kay Yow.

Coach Yow was an amazing coach with not just a Hall of Fame resume, but an even better person with a Hall of Fame personality. I had the opportunity to be an assistant equipment manager for the women's basketball team for 2 seasons. To the average person, the job didn't sound glamorous but it paid half of my tuition, I got to travel with the team, and I got a lot of free basketball gear. It was a great experience that I will cherish forever. I graduated from NC State in 2007, but 2 years later I received a devastating call.

In January of 2009 Coach Yow passed away after battling with breast cancer and I had been invited to her funeral. I tend to shy away from funerals for my own personal reasons, but I made an exception this time.

Funerals are usually very somber events that tend to go on and on with songs and special remarks from family and friends. Her funeral was different. Coach Yow was a big deal in the college basketball world. There were thousands of people there and many famous people from the sports world. I, like many of the other attendees, thought that famous coaches and players would be giving their well wishes and condolences from the pulpit. We were wrong. There was only one speaker, Coach Yow.

The preacher came up and spoke for maybe 5 minutes and then put on a video Coach Yow prepared before she passed away. She talked about many different occurrences in her life involving sports and it was very moving and even entertaining. One of the last things she said shaped the entire philosophy of my life. She said that cancer may have taken her life, but she didn't lose to cancer because everyone in the audience had the opportunity to continue her fight.

She told everyone present that someday her battle would inspire someone to find a cure. She stated that we could even be the person to find a cure. It was a life changing message, and the foundation of what I gathered from her message was: *Refuse to Lose.*

The message in her eulogy was consistent with the life she lived as a Hall of Fame coach. Oftentimes, after losses the players would be upset and Coach Yow would console them by telling them the loss was not about the game on the court, but the game of life.

I distinctly remember hearing one conversation Coach Yow had with a player who made a mistake late in a game that lead to a victory for the other team. The player was crying and upset and Coach Yow calmly stated that none of her teams ever lost a game. She went on to say that if you learn a lesson from losing a game that you can use in your life then that loss was a win.

After hearing Coach Yow's eulogy and thinking back on the times I worked with the team, I began to shape and adopt the *Refuse to Lose* game plan. Ultimately I had to activate this philosophy in my life because I began experiencing a lot of losses. At just 24 years old I went bankrupt. I also failed in numerous entrepreneurial ventures before the age of 25. I was stuck working a job that I did not like in order to make ends meet and I felt like a loser.

Though I heard those powerful words from Coach Yow, I was not living the power of those words on a daily basis. My wife did not work a job because we both decided that having her at home would be the best for our family. This did put a bit of a financial burden on me and I sometimes felt I was letting my family down.

One faithful day, during a short break at work, I went into the bathroom and I looked at myself in the mirror and told myself: **You can do this!**

It was at that point I realized this saying was true, **you're not born a winner or a loser, you are born a chooser**. I give you the identical advice I gave myself that day. **<u>You can do this!</u>** The *Refuse to Lose* game plan is all about gathering the best information to make the best decisions in your life. I made the decision to start my own speaking business and a few short years later I was conducting paid speaking engagements all across the country.

It took a lot of work and I experienced a lot of losses, but most of all, it took the active application of the principles I will share throughout the course of this book. Personally, I always say **I never lose, I either win or I learn.** I may take a defeat, but I will never be defeated. My hope for you is that after you apply the principles displayed in this book, you will begin winning the game of life and making a powerful impact on everyone you come in contact with.

CHAPTER 2
The IMPACT Effect

Playing sports was the ultimate high for me when I was growing up. I played both varsity football and basketball in high school and I was a pretty decent player in both sports. Nothing was more exciting than getting ready for the big games against our rivals. In AAU basketball, the rival teams that come to mind are the Charlotte Nets, the Carolina Hornets, and the Alamance Athletics. In high school our rival teams were easily Dudley, Carver, and Southwest high schools.

We won some games and we lost some games. When we would lose to our rivals I would get sick to my stomach. I hated losing in general, but when I lost to a rival, I hated it even more. Win, lose, or draw, my teammates and I always drew closer, and this is what I overlooked all those years ago.

If we won a game it was the jubilation of a victory that brought me closer to my teammates. If we suffered a heartbreaking loss, we would all come together and bounce back.

In the game of life the only way to truly win is to impact others in a positive way. It doesn't matter if you have a great victory in your personal life or a crushing defeat; you can make a positive impact on others. It's what I call the *IMPACT Effect*.

To best illustrate the principles within the *Refuse to Lose* game plan, the word IMPACT is going to be used as a double entendre. The first meaning of the word impact is simply a positive and powerful influence. Within the scope of the 4 areas I believe all people should win in (faith, fitness, finances, and family) it is always about others.

In order to truly serve people, you have to make an impact on them. The deity and/or religion we subscribe to always includes something outside of ourselves. Our faith also includes a certain community of believers in which we are supposed to live in harmony with. Fitness (both physically and mentally) has to do with our ability to live a higher quality of life to better live and love with others. Having stable finances is important to ensure that we are certain about our ability to provide for ourselves and others.

Finally, our families have everything to do with other people, most namely our relatives and our close friends. We must however, realize the difference between relatives and family; **relatives are those that have your name, family are those that have your back**. When you correctly activate the *Refuse to Lose* game plan and have the subsequent *IMPACT Effect* more people you work with and serve with will feel like family.

Within the confines of these 4 focus areas, we can see how they do not just have an impact on us, but on others too. It would be wise then to ensure that as we grow and accumulate personal achievements, that we do it in a fashion that paves a trail of positive influence. The *IMPACT Effect* means that you bring value to everyone you come into contact with.

The second definition of impact is defined as an acronym. The rest of this book will walk you through the acronym IMPACT and how it relates to winning the game of life. The IMPACT acronym is as follows:

> The **Refuse to Lose** *Game Plan*
>
> **I**-inspiration
> **M**-motivation
> **P**-purpose
> **A**-action
> **C**-courage
> **T**-transformation

In order to win, you need a game plan. As the old adage goes, **those who fail to plan, plan to fail**. The IMPACT acronym is the *Refuse to Lose* game plan. Within these 6 items you will learn how to win in the game of life and positively impact those around you. Whenever you are facing a challenge in any of your 4 focus areas, whenever you feel like you want to quit, or whenever you want to change course, this game plan will help you win and positively impact other people. When you have a positive impact on others you cannot lose. Impacting others lifts you out of the doldrums of depression, defeat, and mediocrity.

Why Should You Utilize This Game Plan?

We live in a skeptical world. Most people don't believe most of what they see on television or read on their smart phones, and you probably should not. I understand that you may have one foot in the skeptic's pool, so let me give you three simple reasons why you should utilize the principles and practices written in this book.

(1) To train your mind.

(2) For the sake of compensation.

(3) For the sake of influence.

To Train Your Mind

The game of life is primarily lost or won in between your ears. Generally speaking, with few exceptions (i.e. a professional athlete, a career blue collar worker, a soldier etc.) you will not have to physically overcome much of anything to obtain success. Even if you do have to be physically stronger, faster, more skilled, etc. the will to do it starts in your mind. So you should utilize the *Refuse to Lose* game plan to ensure you are beginning to train your mind.

I was listening to a hypnotist that said something very interesting. He said that we are all hypnotized in some form or fashion. I personally understood what he was saying, I just would use a different word than hypnotize. I would say that we are all trained or conditioned to do certain things.

James Allen put it this way when he wrote, **a man's mind can be likened to a garden, which may be intelligently cultivated or neglected, it must, and will, bring forth. Weeds come whether or not good seed is present, one must actively labor to annihilate and minimize the weeds.** Reading information like this will help breed the mindset to take action and win in life. It will help hypnotize, brainwash, or condition your mind for ultimate success.

We do what we see repeatedly. **Repetition is the mother of learning**. If you see something over and over again, even if it is the wrong thing, you will ultimately repeat it. This is why people that grow up in abusive households and don't receive proper counseling tend to repeat the actions they grew up seeing as children. Therefore, if you consume what you read in this book it will be a part of the process of training your mind to build a lifestyle of resolve, progression, and achievement. It will train you to have the mindset of a winner.

For the Sake of Compensation

Dr. Martin Luther King, Jr. has a quote that says, **not everyone can be famous, but everyone can be great because greatness is determined by service.** In other words, you may not ever make it on the cover of *People Magazine*, but you can serve people by what you have been given, and by what you can give. Along those same lines I truly believe that though not everyone can be famous, everyone can be paid well for doing what they love and what they are skilled in.

Applying the game plan that will be outlined in this book means that you add immense value to every single person you come in contact with. After you discover the process of turning your skills, experiences, and desires into a commodity then you will be paid highly for your services. Every single highly paid individual that I have encountered utilizes the principles that are written within these pages.

It is my firm belief that when you were placed in your Mother's womb by The Most High, there was an assignment for you to complete. Employing these principles will not only help you build a mindset that will not allow you to falter, these principles will also send you on a search for your special gift.

Your special gift is what you've been given to give to the world. Your special gift is the value you are 'called' to give that will return value back to you if you utilize it properly. The caveat is if you do not answer your call then you will always face a certain level of frustration and a lack of fulfillment in your life.

Back in 2007 before I discovered my calling I was waiting on a 'call.' At that time, I had two jobs that barely paid me $1,800/month combined with no health benefits. The hours were crazy and I was getting more frustrated as each day went by. I applied to work for the Sheriff's Department as a detention officer. If I was hired by the Sheriff's Department, my take home pay after health benefits would be $2,500/month. On top of that I would only have to work 15 days a month. Though it was not where I wanted to be career wise, it represented a better opportunity for me to grow and provide for my family.

When I initially applied, they explained to me that getting hired was a very long process. They explained that I would have two face to face interviews and after the second interview if I was going to be hired, they would call me on a Tuesday to tell me my start date.

Every Tuesday after my second interview I was anxiously waiting on that call. I knew if I received that call that I would be hired and I would be in a better position to reach my goals. Then one Tuesday I got the call! They gave me my start date and I was officially a new hire.

I tell that story because all of us are here for a particular reason and we should be actively seeking out what our calling is. When you find out what your calling is, the excitement level should be at a greater place than mine was when I received the call from the Sheriff's Department. This should be the case because once you find your calling you will know where to start digging for your buried treasure. When you discover your calling it is just like someone handing you a treasure map showing you exactly where your buried treasure is.

I believe it is so important to discover what your calling is that I dedicated an entire book to it entitled

Perfected Passion Produces Prosperity. The book covers several questions you should ask yourself in order to discover your calling. I also covered how one can turn their calling into great compensation. Plain and simple, the *Refuse to Lose* game plan, when applied properly, will allow you to make a great deal of money in your field of choice.

Leaders go where their calling takes them. Think about the wealthiest people you know or know of. The vast majority of them are wealthy because they are operating at a high level in their calling. Your favorite celebrity, professional athlete, business guru, or executive all have a great love for what they do, add immense value to who they serve, and they are operating in their calling. Money isn't everything, but it sure does answer for a lot of things. Someone once said, money can't buy you happiness, but it sure can put a down payment on it. This book will help you with your down payment.

For the Sake of Influence

The final and arguably most important reason you should utilize this game plan is for the sake of influence. People admire and follow those individuals who never quit and strive to win the game of life. On Twitter, music artist Justin Bieber has over 72 million followers.

I am not stating this fact to validate "Bieber Fever," I am pointing this out because Justin Bieber is operating in his calling and is making a huge impact on people that listen to his music. As a result of this, he has tons of influence over people. He could literally send out a tweet asking his followers to follow someone else and almost immediately millions of his followers would follow that person. Influence is the greatest way you can make a positive impact on someone else. If you can influence people, you can help modify their behavior for the better.

I honestly believe that most people are good at their core. There are some evil deviants out there, but the vast majority of people have good things in mind for those around them. When you refuse to succumb to adversity and employ the *Refuse to Lose* game plan in your life, people will follow you because they admire you for what you are able to do.

When I was in college, I made a list of the famous people I wanted to meet. That list was made up of megastars such as Will Smith, Jamie Foxx, Tyler Perry, Justin Timberlake, Magic Johnson, and a few lesser known guys such as Tony Robbins, Les Brown, and Dave Ramsey.

Why were these particular people on my list? They were on my list because I admired them for their prowess and what they have accomplished. All of the men I mentioned are in the upper echelon of their fields and have utilized the *Refuse to Lose* game plan in their own right. The 6 principles presented in this book will teach you how to stand out and make an influence.

These 6 principles will encourage you when everyone else is discouraged. These 6 principles will bequeath the legacy of determination that your forefathers needed to overcome the unknown, the dangerous, and the primitive. After you learn and apply the principles that have been written within these pages, everyone you come into contact with will be drawn to you in such a way that you can make a positive change in their world.

Your desire to win the game of life, make an impact on others, and become successful is really more about your desire to become an agent of influence. When people are influenced by you, then you can easily spread the integrity, good morals, and good works that you represent.

So many people yearn to gain wealth and fame to satisfy their own selfish desires. They *only* want more stuff for themselves or they just want to be seen. I urge you to go against that mentality. It is okay to have lots of stuff and it is okay to be seen, but if you are going to 'win' in the game of life it's going to take more benevolent intentions.

Make sure that as you labor to become a winner in life you keep others in mind, overcome all opposition, and help other people get better. Our lives should influence people to do more, be more, and have more for the betterment of themselves and the betterment of others. In the coming chapters we will be discussing each element in the word IMPACT and ultimately how you go from inspiration to transformation, and how to win the ultimate competition of life.

CHAPTER 3

Inspiration

What lies behind us and what lies before us, are tiny matters compared to what lies within us.

Ralph Waldo Emerson

The game of life can be discouraging, dismantling, filled with trials, and tribulations. The news, social media timelines, and naysayers all want you to go through life afraid of success. With all of the information one can find and gather online comes even more pessimism and skepticism towards life.

How do we overcome this? How do we apply the *Refuse to Lose* game plan to the negative world outside of us? It's simple actually. We take the first letter in the game plan and integrate it into our lives.

The first letter in the word IMPACT is 'I' and it stands for inspiration. Utilizing this component of the game plan is all about getting inspired to become an inspiration and then subsequently sharing inspiration on a daily basis. You should bathe yourself with inspiration just like you bathe your body with water. The sweet taste of inspiration should be present in your mouth every day like the taste of toothpaste is present in your mouth every day to freshen your breath.

What exactly is inspiration? Inspiration is defined as **the process of being mentally stimulated to do something**.

A deeper meaning of the word inspiration deals with the Latin root of the word which is 'spirare.' Spirare means breath. In other words inspiration can be translated to mean 'breath in.' So when you get inspired you get life breathed into you. We all need air to breathe. If you have ever lost your breath you know and understand how crucial it is to live.

Obtaining inspiration as well as giving inspiration can be illustrated using this example. Imagine that you were at dinner and you heard a loud gasp behind you. As you turned around to see what the gasp was all about, you observed a man lying on the ground. It appears that this man has had some sort of cardiac episode.

Following the proper protocol you immediately yell to the other patrons that someone should call 911. You then check the vital signs of the individual. "Oh no," you think to yourself. They have no pulse and they do not appear to be breathing. Immediately you begin performing CPR on the person. Never in your life did you imagine that you would remember the steps, but adrenaline seemed to take over your mind and you recalled every last step.

You start with chest thrusts, then you proceed with giving the person mouth to mouth resuscitation (with a mask of course), and after about 3 breaths they start coughing and their vitals come back to normal.

You are a hero! You literally breathed life into that person! You stimulated that person's breath so they were able to continue their life. Inspiration is the same way. Inspiration is a process that starts outside of you. Inspiration stimulates your feelings and your emotions. Inspiration can breathe life into someone. It is imperative that we utilize something outside of us to help win the game of life.

Many times something outside of us can push us to heights that we never knew existed. Everyone has heard about the tragedy of the Titanic. Of the 705 survivors there is a story about one of the survivors that embodies true inspiration.

As the gigantic vessel began to sink after striking an iceberg, many people were destined to meet their creator. There were over 2,000 people on the boat, but only 20 lifeboats. This left over half of the people on the Titanic with no hope of surviving the sinking ship. Imagine how disheartening that fact would have been to you.

One lifeboat, filled to the brim floated away for a full night with no sign of a rescue boat in sight. The night was so cold that many feared that the frigid temperatures would be their demise. All the individuals huddled together to draw from one another's body heat to survive.

Once the dawn came a passenger on the lifeboat yelled to the others that they saw something, but it wasn't a rescue boat, it was a man floating on what appeared to be a broken piece of driftwood. The person looked extremely ill and had icicles hanging from their nose and mouth.

After the person was lifted onto the lifeboat, one of the passengers asked the man how he survived in such extreme conditions. With his teeth chattering he said, "I promised my 4 year old daughter that I would come home." His inspiration was his daughter. He had something outside of himself to live for. Without the inspiration of his daughter, he may not have survived as long as he did in the arctic water.

Finding inspiration on a daily basis can be a difficult task. Every day we are so enamored in day to day activities that we may not make the time to search for it. Winners find it no matter what.

There are multiple places to find inspiration. There is inspiration in music, on YouTube, in movies, and through words of wisdom via conversations or books. You can also get inspired by doing some sort of physical activity such as cardio or weight training. I urge you to take an inventory of what you listen to, what you read, and who you speak to on a daily basis. If the music you are listening to is degrading, senseless, and reckless, get rid of it. If the movies you watch only stimulate your loins, your fears, or selfish desires, stop watching them. To be a winner in the game of life you have to live every day inspired. Inspiration takes you to another level in life.

Historic events can also inspire you. These types of events may bring back the feelings and attitudes you or others similar to you experienced at that time.

At the time of this writing, the movie "42" has been released. It is the cinematic account of the legendary baseball icon Jackie Robinson and how he heroically became the first black baseball player to play Major

League Baseball. Perhaps reliving that moment in time is something that would inspire you to get over the obstacles you have in your life.

You could also pull from moments in your life where you did something great. I do that to inspire myself when I think back to my days playing basketball in high school.

When I was in high school our heated cross town rival was James B. Dudley High School. Dudley was a national powerhouse in basketball at that time.

It was January of 2001; I was a 15 year old sophomore that thought I could conquer the world. Though we were clearly out matched, I believed that we could beat Dudley. While our confidence was high days leading up to the game, things changed on game day. Some of my teammates peaked out into the arena and saw over 2,000 people packed into a gym that was only supposed to hold 1,200. They got very nervous.

That was when the inspiration we needed walked into the locker room in the form of our assistant coach. Our coach always gave us a pep talk before games, but in that particular pep talk, he took it to another level. I still remember his words.

"Gentlemen! Today is the day that you seize your moment! We will not let Dudley come into our house and beat us. Do you know what that's like? That's like them kicking down our front door, kicking us out of our favorite chair, taking the remote to our TV, drinking our Kool-Aid, and taking our women! Are we going to let them do that?"

Despite the strange commentary up to that point we all instinctively yelled, "NO!" By that time, we had all huddled around him and our coach instructed us to put our hands on top of one another. My coach then continued.

"Gentlemen, the people want the underdog to succeed! The people want you to win! So on three, I want you to say give the people what they want, 1-2-3---" "Give the people what they want!!!"

I will be honest, at that moment I didn't really understand what he was talking about. I mean really, favorite chairs? Kool-Aid? Taking our women? It was crazy, but it got us so excited and inspired that we went out there and played a great game.

We won the game at the buzzer, and from that game on we always broke our huddles with 'Give the people what they want,' because it reminded us of a time when we were able to do something that we didn't think we could do. It reminded us of the competitive spirit we displayed that day, and reminded us to compete. Inspiration simply reminds of the greatness we can all have and share. Inspiration reminds us of the greatness within every single one of us. Inspiration is the spark that causes us to compete with life knowing we can win. I invite you to compete every single day. Be inspired.

The gifts inside of each and every one of us are so powerful that we can overcome and endure anything. If you are going to win in the game of life you must be inspired. The enemy of greatness wants you defeated. If you are continually inspired, you can overcome those tough times when you face discouragement and disappointment. Those who endeavor to be great are those that face the greatest obstacles. Do you want to be great? If your answer is yes, then you should be prepared for a ton of obstacles.

I will reiterate, life is a game that you only win if you positively impact other people. When you win others win, and if you don't win, some people won't win. Another way to inspire yourself is to think about the people who will do well when you do well. You have more people looking at you than you realize.

Become an Inspiration

When I decided to leave my job back in 2013 it was scary. I was shocked however, when I discovered I inspired some of my co-workers. After some of my co-workers found out that I put in my two weeks' notice to resign they came up to me during my lunch and said things like, "I've always looked up to you," or, "I've always wanted to start my own business, how'd you do it?"

Many of these people were individuals that I didn't know outside of work, but for some reason they saw something in me. What you need to realize is that **people do not see you through their eyes; they see you through your eyes, and they are watching you.**

Not only do you need to be inspired to win in life, but you should become an inspiration as well. One of the greatest skills you can learn in life is the skill of inspiring people. Remember, inspiration is about your feelings. A huge part of inspiration is arousing positive emotion. In addition to that, inspiration is a great way to encourage your colleagues, classmates, associates, friends, and family during the tough times they may be going through. If you can master the art of inspiration, you will never lose in life.

You never know what trials the people in your life face when they are not around you. Everyone faces times when things are not going their way. Everyone has to stare in the cold ugly face of disappointment, tragedy, and setbacks at some point in their life. Your job as a victorious participant in this game called life is to ensure that the people who come into contact with you continually see inspiration to battle their disappointments.

Disappointment often becomes a part of our everyday life to the point that we get familiar with it and even come to expect it. If you come to expect disappointment, more often than not disappointment will show up. There is a term called the law of expectation which says that our expectation is stronger than our desire.

More plainly, the law of expectation says that we get in life what we expect in our heart, not what we want in our mind. So do not expect to get disappointed, no matter how often you have been in the past because if you do, disappointment will continue to show up in your future.

Dealing with disappointment is a 'discouragement' thing, but conquering disappointment is an 'inspiration' thing. By being an inspiration to others, you have the opportunity to resuscitate the lifelessness that comes from disappointment in someone else's life. Disappointment occurs when an expectation goes unmet.

Have you ever been stood up before? If you have, odds are you have been disappointed. Have you ever received a bad grade on a test, an assignment, or an evaluation? If you have, odds are you have been disappointed.

The skill of inspiring others is one that can come easily to different types of people. To become an inspiration, you first have to realize that though you are on a mission to win in your life, change the world for the better, and become the person you are destined to be, others may not receive you well.

You must realize that some pitiful souls will repel the light you attempt to put into their dark lives. The vast majority of individuals that you will encounter will not have your drive, your desire, or your awareness of what they are supposed to accomplish. Do not allow their playing small in life to cause you to shrink. This is where true competition comes into play. What do you do when you smile and say good morning to someone and they roll their eyes in response?

You have to continue to stay inspired and kill their discouraging spirit with how you carry yourself. There are a lot of different ways you can walk, talk, and be an inspiration to others. Here are four quick fun things you can do to be an inspiration to those around you:

- Wear an inspiring t-shirt or wristband.

- Give away free inspiring novelties such as CDs, customizable fortune cookies at the office.

- Celebrate the individuals you serve with.

- Encourage others around you to think about the next level as often as possible.

These are just four ideas that you can activate quickly. Can you add more to the list? These little things will add a ray of light to people's lives. These things will also help activate the Baader-Meinhof Phenomenon or the frequency illusion. Have you ever bought a new car and seen the new car at every street corner after your purchase? That's the Baader-Meinhof Phenomenon. You see your car not because everyone copied you and bought your car, it's because the make, model, and color of your car is at the top of your mind. So in essence by activating some of the ideas presented in this chapter you can help people keep inspiration at the top of their mind.

Life will offer plenty of things that will discourage and dishearten the people you work with. By continually being inspired and sharing inspiration, you make it easier for you to win in life. You also facilitate the opportunity for others to know that they too can win. Since inspiration comes from outside of you, keep seeking ways to be inspired every day. As an inspiration make it a point to inspire someone by being the winner you truly are.

Game Plan Review

- Stay inspired daily.

- Listen to inspirational music when you wake up and when you are discouraged.

- Limit disempowerment and enhance empowerment.

- Look back to historic events in your life and in the world and draw inspiration from them.

- Think about the people that would benefit from you winning the game of life.

- Inspire others using the 4 ideas given at the end of the chapter to activate the Baader-Meinhof Phenomenon.

CHAPTER 4

Motivation

Inspiration is about how you feel; motivation is about what you see.

The second letter in IMPACT is 'M' which stands for motivation. Many have the idea that inspiration and motivation are the same thing. They are not. I admit that they are similar, and in the family of words they may be first cousins, but they are not the same. When I was younger, my coach used to use a small dry erase clipboard to draw up out of bounds plays on the sideline. The plays worked to perfection 100% of the time on the clipboard. We then had to transfer what we saw on the clipboard into what we did on the court. We had to have vision.

In order to start a fire you need a match, or a lighter of some sort. You need something to ignite the fire. For the boy scouts and camping aficionados reading, you know that you may be able to start a fire, but you need more than just a spark to keep the fire going.

Motivation is what keeps the fire going. It is the oxygen to the fire, without oxygen a fire cannot burn continually. In school we learned that grease fires cannot be quenched with water, they have to be smothered because without oxygen a fire cannot survive.

Let's look back to the CPR example we used in the previous chapter on inspiration. Your part in the CPR experience stimulated the breathing process as well as the heartbeat, but after you stimulated those vital signs you backed away and allowed nature to operate. Motivation is essential if you want to win the game of life.

You don't have to be motivated to be a regular person. You have to be motivated if you want to be a winner. There must be something inside of you that desires the incredible to happen for you. Motivation comes from within.

Inspiration is the movement of outward emotions, but motivation is the movement of the mundane. Inspiration is the key that ignites the engine of success; motivation is the battery and the alternator that keeps things going under the hood. Without what is underneath the hood, the car is no good to anyone.

Hopefully, you have a better idea of the differences between inspiration and motivation so that we can now move forward into how you can become more motivated. As a professional speaker, I am often called a 'motivational' speaker when in actuality the more appropriate title is an 'inspirational' speaker. This title is more suited because speakers cannot keep people motivated. As you navigate the game of life, you cannot lose sleep or gain worry because others are not motivated.

Motivation is your inner will. Motivation is all about the reason behind your action. Motivation is also our ability to get over obstacles and less than ideal circumstances to achieve. Motivation is the essence of the *Refuse to Lose* game plan. Most people are not motivated individuals. Most people get inspired, but after their inspiration fizzles out they cannot keep going. That cannot be your swansong.

When the word motivation comes up, the words; will power, determination, resolve, persistence, and the like probably come to mind; there's nothing fancy about motivation. It is the grit, the grime, and the foundation for winners. It is the beautiful truth behind every success story. Motivation is the late hours, the failure, the pressure, the setbacks, the early mornings, the tears, and the million dollar dream despite an empty bank account. It is the dirt that nourishes the seeds of success that you have to water with the light of inspiration.

The difficult thing about being motivated is that motivation is your will to do something. You have to be willing to do something before you actually do it. In order to be supremely motivated I suggest removing too much thought and begin developing a system for execution. Instead of putting conditions on what you want to do, systematize the steps that lead you to your goal.

In his outstanding book *The Compound Effect*, Darren Hardy breaks down an interesting way for people to grow and achieve. His major premise is that we should all start with very simple steps to become successful. An example he uses is if you state that you want to achieve a certain goal of losing weight; instead of joining a fancy gym and getting on a tough to follow diet plan, he suggests that you take one small step toward weight loss.

Hardy gives an example of a woman in his office that wanted to lose weight and run a marathon. His suggestion to her was to simply start by taking the stairs every day at work. Most people try to do too much too soon; therefore they are only inspired and not motivated. If the first step is not relatively easy then your motivation will not last.

The key component to motivation is having a tangible and practical goal. Without goals you can have no motivation. One of my mentors once said, **if you lack motivation, you have yet to see the potential of your future.** Your goals should give you a glimpse of your future. Here's the system for setting goals that can motivate you: (1) Understand and know that you cannot lose if you don't quit, (2) Think who/what/why, (3) Write it down, (4) Take the first step.

It is that simple. When you think 'who,' get a picture of a person or people that stand to win when you win. Find their picture on social media or in your photo album and print it out and put it on a bulletin board. When you think 'what' think of what you want to accomplish. This is where you have the latitude to be a bit materialistic. I am of the mindset that people often need something shallow to motivate them.

Many times when I tell my story to audiences, they marvel at how I managed to find time to write books and build my speaking business while working a full-time job in a relatively quick manner. I often respond by saying that my wife Sierra was a motivating factor.

I have a wonderful wife who loves me and would do anything for me. To convince my wife to marry me I told her that being with me would be one of the best decisions she ever made. I told her that she would have a house, a car, and would not have to work a job if she didn't want to.

Well in 2007 when I was a broke college graduate, I had to work a job I hated to keep my promise. Had it not been for Sierra, I would not have worked in a jail. After working in the jail for a while they began to cut our pay. Sooner or later Sierra would have had to get a job, so I was motivated to ramp up my efforts to build my business and quit altogether to pursue my dreams full-time.

I felt motivated to leave my job in order to expand my income and grow my business so that my Queen could continue to stay at home and do what she desired. Initially I was motivated to work a job I disliked because of my wife. I hated working at the jail, but my 'why' was so much greater than my discomfort. I was afraid to quit my job because of the chance it would not work, but my 'why' was bigger than my 'what ifs.' To be motivated your reason 'why' and your ability to overcome must coalesce to obtain results.

The Common Denominator of Success

In order to be motivated, you have to check your

why often and utilize the common denominator of success. The common denominator of success is making a habit of doing things that unsuccessful people refuse to do. You should highlight the word, *habit*. We are creatures of habit. **We are not products of our environments; we are all products of our habits.** A habit is defined as a settled or regular tendency or practice, especially one that is hard to give up.

Habits are things that we do regularly. When you make a habit of doing things that unsuccessful people refuse to do, you regularly practice what successful people do. In order to build a habit you have to first consciously do something that is not regularly practiced.

If you get on a weight training program in order to gain muscle or lose fat, odds are that the program is going to have a set workout schedule and diet regimen. Initially, you will have to consciously refer to the literature that you have in order to ensure you are doing things the right way. The program may tell you that you have to work out 4 times a week and only have a cheat day in your diet once a month.

Perhaps before you started the weight training program you worked out once a week and you had a cheat day every day. If this is the case you will have to consciously set out to do what the training program says.

The real motivation occurs when you face opposition. What happens when you go to your favorite restaurant that has your favorite dessert, but it's not a cheat day? What do you do? Right then and there you have to look at the reason why you are on that training program, and if the reason is not large enough you will succumb to your dominating habit of eating whatever you want.

This is a big reason why most people cannot win in life. Most people are used to doing things that unsuccessful people do. The same things that unsuccessful people do not like to do are the same things that successful people also naturally do not like to do. Right now it is Friday around 1pm and I am typing away at my computer.

It is a beautiful day outside and honestly I would rather be outside enjoying the weather or watching one of my favorite shows on my DVR. It is a lot more comfortable for me to give in to my desires of pleasure than it is for me to be disciplined.

The danger is that **pleasures without practice places us in a plateau**. Most people who are not successful simply do not practice forming successful habits. They focus on pleasures instead of practice. For you to utilize the common denominator of success, you must first gain a big enough reason why.

Why do you want to be successful? Earlier in the book I gave you three major reasons to follow the *Refuse to Lose* game plan.

However, those are three reasons that motivate people in general. I do believe that most people can be motivated by those three reasons, but it is what lies within those reasons that will really motivate you.

Why do you want to be wealthy? Why do you want to influence others? If it isn't wealth and influence what is it? Did you promise your parents you would take care of them when they were older? The reason why you want to win is arguably the most important reason why you will win. When your 'why' is big enough, the 'how tos' will fall into place. You should compile a list of goals for yourself and put them where you can look at them on a daily basis.

Your subconscious mind does not know the difference between fantasy and reality. All it knows are commands. If you continually visit your goals by looking at them and commanding your success, then your brain will develop a path for your feet to get to them. It is a fact that what we focus on gets bigger.

The next way you can motivate yourself is by finding out what industry or profession you want to win in. You can have all the ambition in the world, but **misplaced ambition leads to frustration.**

For the better part of my teenage years I wanted to be a professional basketball player. Once I realized that I would never become one and focused on discovering what I would win in, then my efforts and focus shifted to that. Some people spend too long chasing things that are not meant for them which causes them to be frustrated, and not motivated.

Focus on finding your passion; **perfected passion produces prosperity**. Your passion or your calling is where you are supposed to standout while you are alive. When you discover where you are supposed to be, it is a lot easier to be motivated there.

Before I became a full-time speaker, there were multiple times that I wanted to give up completely. What helped me stay motivated was the fact that I was continually getting validation from others because of my speaking programs.

Things were tough and at times it was difficult to be motivated. I recalled times when I would get off of work from my job at the jail on a Tuesday evening, jump on a plane Wednesday morning and speak Wednesday afternoon. Then I would hop on a plane Thursday morning, get home, and then go work nightshift. More often than not however, after I completed a presentation, the attendees would give me great compliments, tweet my quotes, buy my books, and recommend me to others.

Those kind words gave me confirmation and allowed me to stay motivated, because they were quiet whispers that told my spirit that I was operating in my calling. Your calling or your passion will motivate you when you are operating in it. When you discover where you are supposed to be operating, it becomes easier to stay motivated.

Another great way to be motivated is to reward yourself for reaching certain milestones. This is a bit tricky because the incentive has to be great enough to move you even when you do not feel like being moved. If you were anything like me when I was in high school, there were many days that I did not want to go to school at all.

My parents, for lack of better words 'inspired' me to get out of the bed and go to school. When I went off to college, however, my parents were not there. The only motivation I had was that if I missed class, it hurt my grade.

When you are in school, the benefit of getting good grades motivates you. When you are working a job, the paycheck you receive motivates you. If you can discover how to reward yourself in a way that pushes you then you will stay motivated. Though these things are outside of us, our desire to achieve them (good grades, money etc.) is deep within.

We are motivated when we assign greater value to our reason for acting than we do to our reason for not acting. Winners in the game of life make sure that they assign great value to the reward of becoming the best in their field of choice. Not only that, but they choose to be motivated to engage their community. A community is a group of people that live, work, or convene in one area. Millions of people want to lose weight primarily for health and vanity. Vanity, although a bit shallow, can move people.

A final note on motivating yourself is that the 'why' should connect to your purpose and something you can measure in time. We will discuss purpose in great detail in the next chapter. If you are looking to change a habit or you want to see a substantial change in something I suggest you give it about 6 weeks. **A goal without a deadline is simply a wish.** Wishes only motivate genies and genies don't exist.

Motivating Others

When you choose to be motivated, those that are around you will take notice and either follow you or get out of the way. What you have to understand is that you cannot motivate other people to do anything. You can inspire them and also give them reasons to be motivated, but only they can choose if they want to press towards a particular mark. When you think of the word motivation think of the word 'movement.' If you are motivated you will display movement. Motivation comes from within. Your landlord can give you a reason to pay the rent on time by threatening to evict you, but if you are not motivated to earn the money to pay your rent then you will be left without a place to stay.

Winning the game of life is a team effort. You need other motivated people around you to win. Let's discuss how to help motivate people.

If you really want others around you to be motivated then encourage them to find out why they are significant. **One thing that every human being desires is significance.** We all want to feel like we matter.

Furthermore, people are always tuned into WIIFM radio station (What's in it for me). In order to get others motivated you have to show them what is in it for them. Sit down and have a personal meeting with all of the people you lead and help them discover their motivation.

Ask them how they want to be remembered. Ask them what makes them feel important. Probe and discover what makes them tick. Why are they working in your office? Why are they a part of your organization? Why are they in your life? Is it a stepping stone? This is an assessment that can be done with family, business associates, co-workers, employees, or anyone in your life. **Life is a team sport**. You need people around you that are motivated.

Another way to motivate others is to connect their motivation to yours. If you are a manager of a corporation, it is pretty simple to connect the two. All you have to do is mention their paycheck and how a more efficient and effective company makes for a more sustainable paycheck. If you are a part of a community, organization or an organization at a school, then their motivation will be more hidden, but it should be easy to find.

More than likely, if someone is involved with work that they do not get compensated for, then their motivation is different than money. Are they on the team to build their resume? Are they on the team because of tradition or obligation? Find out their motivation and connect it to your motivation and make it a point to tell them that you will do everything you can to help them reach their goals.

Winners in the game of life are constantly reminding everyone around them of the next level. Use your inner will. **Winners look at obstacles as something to get them going, losers look at obstacles as something to get them gone.** Don't ever give up. You can only lose if you quit. Failure is not final nor is it fatal. In the words of Og Mandino in his book *The Greatest Salesman in the World,* **failure will never overtake you if your determination to succeed is strong enough**. Let your determination outlast your failures.

Game Plan Review

- Ask yourself: Why do you want to be successful, prosperous, and influential?

- Be willing to do what unsuccessful people are not willing to do.

- Reward yourself when you make steps towards your goals.

- Write down your goals to constantly remind yourself of what they are, and why they are important.

- To get others motivated, get to know them, find their motivation, and connect your motivation to theirs.

- Never give up.

CHAPTER 5

Purpose

When the purpose of a thing is unknown, abuse is inevitable. Dr. Myles Munroe

The 'P' in IMPACT stands for purpose. This may be one of the most important components of the game plan. Purpose is the reason behind your motivation. Your 'why' keeps you motivated. The intention behind your action takes you from motivation to greatness. In the chapter on motivation, we discussed willingness, determination, and having goals. This chapter will discuss the intent behind what you are willing and determined to do.

Inspiration gets you excited to move in the right direction. Motivation keeps you going despite the obstacles you may face. Purpose is the deep meaning behind why you are inspired and motivated. Purpose is the ultimate intent of your life. John Maxwell said **the person who forgets the ultimate is a slave to the immediate.**

Earlier we used the analogy of a car key being a car's inspiration or the thing that ignited or stimulated the car to start. Motivation was the battery and the alternator. Purpose is the reason why the car was created, and what it works to do. Some people are motivated and inspired to do the wrong things. What good is it to win the game of life if you have evil and destructive intentions?

The quote at the beginning of the chapter really struck a chord with me when I first heard it. When the purpose of a thing is not known then that thing will ultimately be abused. The purpose of a car is for ground transportation to go from point A to point B. That's what it was designed for. If someone thought a car was created for water transportation then the car's purpose would be abused.

The same goes for you and me. If we do not understand why we were created then we will be inspired and motivated for the wrong reasons. Jails and prisons all over the world are filled with people who were inspired and motivated to do the wrong things.

If you have ever been in a relationship that you were

mistreated in the person doing the mistreating did not understand the purpose of your relationship. Individuals who forget or never discover the reason why they were created will eventually abuse their lives.

Let's look at this scenario for more clarification. If a man bought his wife a gift and it was not her birthday, their anniversary, or a special holiday, you might think that the man was being a good husband. Certainly his wife would post pictures of this great gift on social media which would cause others to reply and comment things like #RelationshipGoals. Many people would envy their great connection from the outside looking in.

However, if it was uncovered that this man was caught cheating on his wife and was buying a gift in order to win her back then you may not think that he was such a good husband. Why? Because of the purpose the gift carried.

The purpose of the gift was to soften her anger towards him, not to augment a flourishing love. In other words, doing good things with the wrong purpose can still end up being a knock on your character. This is one of the biggest points you need to gather from knowing your purpose. Someone's purpose tells more about the individual than the actual deed in itself. To truly change the world by what you become, you have to know and understand your purpose.

Don't misunderstand me here, I want you to win. I want you to compete. I want you to become successful, wealthy, happy, and help other people do the same. What I do not want is for you to do all of these things and become a terrible person. I want you to desire wealth to provide for your family and others that are less fortunate. I want you to gain an education so that you can help enrich the world. Like the good book says, **for what does it profit a man to gain the whole world and forfeit his soul?**

I would be remiss if I told you that knowing your purpose is critically important, but did not tell you what your purpose was. The definition of purpose that I am about to give you is of paramount importance. It is like the bottom line of the bottom line. We talked about the purpose of a car before being created to transport people from one destination to another on the ground.

It does not matter if the car is a Lexus or a Toyota, an Acura or a Honda, a Chevrolet or a Cadillac. All cars have the same purpose. The same is true for things in nature. A bumblebee was created to pollinate flowers. That's its purpose. It does not matter if the bumblebee buzzes loud, if it is really big and flies slow or really small and flies fast. The purpose of one bumblebee is the same as any other bumblebee. Every species has a specific purpose.

The same goes for us as human beings. We were all created with the same overarching purpose. **Our purpose in life is to give the world a glimpse of Heaven, by what we do, what we have, and who we are**. Consider highlighting that definition, tweeting it, Facebook posting it, creating an E-card, a meme and Instagraming it because it is truly that important. To sum it up, **our purpose is to perpetuate goodness.**

Even if you are not a religious or spiritual person, you visualize positive things when you think of the word Heaven. The words people associate with Heaven are that of streets of gold, mansions, joy forevermore, no sorrow, perfect weather, and a perfect world. It is the ultimate pinnacle of goodness.

The Creator created us to glorify Him and spread His glory. For some odd reason, He decided to give us free will. This means that we can choose to do whatever we want to do with our lives.

Going back to the foundational quote in the beginning of the chapter, if we do not know our purpose then ultimately we will abuse our lives. Why do people do senseless and terrible things? They lose sight of their purpose.

When you really understand that you were put here to perpetuate good and give the world a snapshot of Heaven, then you will begin operating your life as a winner in all aspects of life. Helen Keller said **one can never consent to creep when one feels an impulse to soar.**

After learning your purpose, you will not be able to settle for anything less than victory in life. You cannot play small any longer by knowing that your purpose is to give the world a glimpse of Heaven. Failure should not be an option for someone who understands his or her underlying reason for being on this planet amongst the living.

There are a lot of people that succeed and scores of them long to give back. Some do it because of how it will make them look, but many genuinely want to give back to others because it is in everyone's DNA to want to do good for others. That is why earlier on in the book I spoke about why you should want to adopt the *Refuse to Lose* game plan and make an impact. Those three reasons again are: to train your mind, for the sake of compensation, and for the sake of influence.

Margaret Thatcher, a legendary British politician has a quote I want to pull a principle from. She said, **no one would remember the Good Samaritan if he'd only had good intentions; he had money as well.** If you do not know the parable of the Good Samaritan from the Bible I will give you a short summary of it.

There was a Jewish man who was attacked, robbed,

beaten badly, and left for dead on the side of the road. Two people passed by him and did not help him. Those two individuals were a Levite and a priest. Both individuals worked in the Temple and were amongst The Most High's chosen people.

A third person then journeyed down the road the man was on, this man was a Samaritan. Unlike the previous two men the Samaritan helped the injured man, put him on his donkey and took him to a local inn. The Samaritan gave the innkeeper money to cover the beaten man's stay and informed the innkeeper that he would pay whatever other expenses the man accrued when he returned from his trip.

This parable was a big deal because Samaritans and Jews did not get along, and the moral of the story is that everyone is our neighbor and we have to love our neighbor as we love ourselves. The quote stated by Margaret Thatcher brings up an irrefutable point. If the Samaritan did not have the money to pay for the beaten man to stay at the inn, his intent to help would've been limited by his resources.

Herein rests the reason why you have to win in the area of your finances. The quicker you are able to do this, the quicker you can start making money to better serve your purpose. **Most, if not all of your goals and**

dreams can be achieved more easily with the aid of more money.

Having more money makes you more of what you are and allows you to more easily serve your purpose. If you do not know and acknowledge your purpose, you allow evil to creep in your life. The Boston marathon bombing, Sandy Hook Elementary shooting, 9/11, the Charleston church killings, and other horrific events were executed by individuals who did not understand their purpose.

When you know that it is your duty to perpetuate good, then your actions will be good. Your purpose will be displayed by what you do. Be intentional about doing good things for others especially when things are not going well for you. Even when your life is a mess, it should eventually turn into a message for someone else to do better when faced with similar obstacles.

Knowing that you were created for good will get you thinking higher thoughts. Higher thoughts will in turn allow you to make better decisions. **Decisions shape destinies.** You will decide to be inspired every day. You will decide to be motivated every day. Once you make these decisions, then those around you will be more driven by their purpose.

Share Your Purpose

Every human being's purpose is the same. We are here to perpetuate good. As a leader and as a winner in life you have to share your purpose with those you work and live around. It is critical that everyone understands that they are here for the greater good.

Not just for the good of themselves, but for the good of others as well. I have three simple strategies you can employ in order to share your purpose. (1) Share the quote about purpose with your team. (2) Find stories about people who get blessed (become wealthy, successful, famous) from doing good deeds for others. (3) Do things to randomly help your micro-community or your team. Let's cover each strategy individually.

Words are powerful. Words have the potential to brighten someone's day or darken it. Words allow us to interpret life and navigate through feelings. Words give us meaning and perspective. When you tell someone that they have been created to give the world a glimpse of Heaven they will automatically respond.

People love great quotes. If you can creatively spread the message of purpose to your teammates, they will be grateful. The definition of purpose as it is defined in this chapter was dropped into my lap one day as I was praying. Once I began adding it to my presentations it quickly became the most quoted, tweeted, and posted quote that my audiences would mention. Your team will love the fact that they are called to do great things to propel themselves forward.

The second strategy for sharing your purpose with others is to find great stories about people who are blessed because of good things they have done. A few years ago, an incredible story was going viral all over the web about a man named Charles Ramsey. The story of Charles Ramsey is one of heroism and great courage.

In short, Ramsey rescued three women who had been kidnapped and held captive for 10 years. When he was asked whether or not he would take a reward, he replied, "Give it to the women, I have a job." Ramsey was a very animated individual in his interviews (search YouTube to see what I mean), but in one word, he was a hero. Showing your teammates this type of story can help show them their purpose.

Seeing is believing, so if your team can see that other people are perpetuating good and gaining benefits from their purpose, they will be more likely to follow suit. Here you will see the frequency illusion resurface. People will constantly be more aware of their purpose and be more likely to activate it in their lives.

The last strategy for helping to spread purpose is to help the people in your micro-community. Your micro-community is made up of the people that you live and work with on a regular basis. So individuals in your family, on your job, at your school, and others that you have direct contact with all qualify.

There are tons of entrepreneurs who do philanthropy on a grand scale. Everyone should want to give as much as they can to help others. What is often overlooked however, are the great things we can do for those in our inner circle. Many times we overvalue what we should do for others, but undervalue what we should for those we come into contact with on a daily basis. We all could use help in some form or fashion. There are times that we receive help and don't even need it, but we never forget it.

One evening around late December, I was in line at Wendy's with my wife and my oldest daughter. Our daughter had just turned three at the time and was being very disruptive. In order to avoid a commotion my wife took her to the car. There was a gentleman in front of us wearing a UPS shirt and I noticed he was looking our way with a smirk.

Once my wife and daughter went back to the car he started a conversation with me. "How old is your daughter?" he asked. "She just turned three," I responded. He smiled and replied, "I know all about that, I've got 4 children. The oldest is 12 then I have an 8 year old, 6 year old, and a 2 year old. So I know exactly what you're going through."

We continued some more small talk and then it was his time to order. What ensued after he ordered truly made an impact on me. He told the cashier that he would pay for whatever I ordered. I was pleasantly shocked by his sentiment and took him up on his offer.

After I received my food I saw that the gentleman was sitting down with someone else and I asked him if he had a card or something so I could return the favor in the near future. He simply said, "You are fine. I am just glad to have been a blessing to you and your family." A complete stranger bought my family and I a meal for no reason other than he wanted to do a good deed. What's cool about this is about a year or so later I was able to return the favor to the same gentleman. I will never forget his kindness, but it was also a reminder to me that I could do that for someone in my family.

Think of one of your grandparents, aunts, uncles, or others who you just want to cheer up. Buy them a meal or pay for their groceries if you can. I encourage you to share your purpose by randomly partaking in acts of kindness within your micro-community. If you are unsure where or when to help people, let me remind you of ever present opportunities. People could always use help with: food, a difficult assignment or project, or payment for something.

If you randomly give someone a free meal, help on something that will move them forward, or some money, your purpose will be shared. People will remember you, but more importantly they will be more inclined to do the same thing for others.

Game Plan Review

- Know that you are here to give the world a glimpse of Heaven and perpetuate good.

- Know that becoming successful is not all for you, but it is for others too.

- Do good without expecting anything in return.

- To make sure your teammates (micro-community) understand purpose do three things: (1) Creatively give them the definition of purpose, (2) Share stories about people who are blessed by doing good, and (3) Do good for them without asking for anything in return.

CHAPTER 6

Action

After it's all said and done a lot more would have been said than done. Mark Twain

The 'A' in IMPACT stands for action. Throughout this book, we have gone over multiple actions you can take to win the game of life. So when you look at the title of this chapter you may be thinking, 'to what type of action is he referring?'

The 'Action' in IMPACT stands for more of a to-do list than a group of attitudes to adopt as previous chapters have stated. There is a saying that goes like this; **hard work beats talent, when talent refuses to work hard.** In life we are all blessed with talents and natural abilities. If we do not couple those talents and abilities with incremental actions on a daily basis, then they will not serve us to the level in which they should.

We will discuss 3 specific actions that you should take immediately to bring about the greatest change. When you take massive action on the steps outlined in the coming pages, your life, your relationships, your organization, and your world will never be the same.

Win the Day

When I worked with the women's basketball team Coach Yow would often say, "Win this possession!" She and her staff broke down the games into possessions. In Division I college basketball, teams play two 20 minute halves. After the 16 minute mark, the 12 minute mark, the 8 minute mark, and the 4 minute mark there is a break in action called a media timeout.

After a win or a loss Coach Yow and her staff would review the game tape and break up the number of possessions within the media timeouts. Once they did this they would have a very accurate count of the number of possessions a successful game produced. In practice she would always tell her players to win each possession. When the team was on the offensive side of the ball a victorious possession would be to take a good shot within the offensive game plan.

On the defensive side of the ball, a successfully won possession was when the opposing team did not score or they scored on a very difficult shot. If the players could focus on pouring their effort into one possession at a time, then Coach Yow's thought process was that they would be a championship team. I believe that in order to win big, we must first win small. As the saying goes, **small hinges swing big doors. Your small hinge or action is to win the day.**

This is something that anyone can do at any station in life. The best way to ensure you are able to win the day is to establish what a victorious day looks like. Earlier we discussed 4 areas in life that everyone should strive to win in; again they include: Faith, family, fitness, and finances. Winning in life is a game of chess, not checkers. It is a game that we must be strategic about in all aspects if we are to win. We have to plan our victories. Start today. Start with one aspect of your life and build on it.

For example, if you want to win in your faith, resolve to read one chapter from your faith book per day and take notes on it. A win in your family life may be to read a story with your kids or call a friend or a loved one. Winning in your physical fitness may be to exercise for 20 minutes in a day or not to eat sweets. In addition to that, a win in the area of mental fitness may be to write down your feelings in a journal. Finally, winning in your finances may be as simple as doing something extra at your job or putting some money away to pay off a debt. You must define what a victorious day is and then go about winning that day. Take this action today.

Define what a winning day is for you and then win. To make it easier perhaps you should start off small and record one win in one aspect. For example, you might say, today I will work out, and once you complete your exercise, you can count it as a win. Then continue to accumulate small wins, until they grow into large victories.

Wake Up with a Sense of Urgency

When you are asleep you are in a different state of consciousness. Your heart rate and breathing slows down. Your hearing is minimal and you are transported into another realm. When you are asleep you are not aware of your surroundings unless something or someone causes you to wake up.

Have you ever been sleeping really hard only to wake up and realize that you slept through your alarm clock? There were numerous times in college where I faced this identical scenario. Upon realizing that I was terribly late I would hurriedly put on some clothes, wipe the crust out of our eyes, and quickly brush my teeth.

I could literally get ready in about 5 minutes and be on my way to class when I woke up late. What is interesting about that scenario is that when my alarm would wake me up at my regular time, I would take a lot longer than 5 minutes to get ready.

The same sentiment holds true for many of our lives today. If you want to win in life you have to 'wake up' and then have a sense of urgency. Waking up in this sense means to become aware of what you are to do while you're here.

Once you wake up from sleeping, you automatically begin to think about what you are going to do with your day. In order to win the game of life a big action step for you is to take is to 'wake up' or find what you love to do with a sense of urgency.

Jim Rohn said something I want to elaborate on. He said, **without a sense of urgency, desire loses its value.** If you don't have a sense of urgency, then your desire or your zeal to accomplish a goal will depreciate in value. It's called the law of diminishing intent. Think about it like this, if you continually procrastinate to take winning actions, your desire to win will diminish. In order to avoid the law of diminishing intent you have to make sure that you have a sense of urgency in your efforts. Here are some ways to make sure you wake up with a sense of urgency:

- Set a deadline for discovering what you love to do. It is a process, but set a deadline of 2 weeks to find what it is you love to do, and then check your progress.

- As it relates to finding what you love to do make a list of things to do every day so you don't waste time.

- Once you find out what you love to do, do it! Do it for free or give samples away as often as possible.

Whether you are focused on your formal education or your current career, having a sense of urgency about discovering what you love to do can profit you. If you want to win the game of life you must discover your passion as soon as possible.

Creating a list of things to do will help you get all of the things you need to do in the proper order. Once you have them in a particular order, you can take the correct action at the appropriate time.

Build a Winning Team

When we discussed inspiration I told you about the epic speech my basketball coach gave my team. I want to use the very same saying he gave us that night as a call to action to begin building a winning team. Giving the people what they want is something that all winners have to do. We don't just win for ourselves, we win for the people. The question is how do we take this action?

When I was unhappy slaving away as a detention officer, I noticed a commonality with many of the young black inmates. The vast majority of them claimed that they were involved in a gang. I never understood why joining a gang was so appealing. I decided to start an unofficial poll of different inmates I came into contact with and asked them two questions, "Why would you join a gang? It only ends in death or prison right?" Many of their answers were typical, but one inmate in particular gave me an answer that stunned me, he simply said: "Out in that world, all I've got is my gang."

It was at that moment I realized that most of the guys I supervised didn't join a gang to rape, kill, pillage, and plunder. They joined a gang because they wanted to be a part of a family. To say it another way, they wanted to be a part of a team. As warped as their intentions and desires might appear, that is something we all have in common. We all want to be on a team because we all have the desire to be significant.

So when I say, give the people what they want, I do not mean that you need to cater to every beckon call of each person you come into contact with. I mean that for you to win in life, you need to build a team. This is an action you cannot ignore.

In order to build a team you must learn how to recruit and retain people. In order to properly recruit people you have to learn the skill of networking. Most people get networking all wrong. Networking is usually seen as a business card collecting activity at a job fair or a trade show. There are four components to networking that I want to point out. First, there is meeting people, and then you must build rapport, next you should gather their contact information, and finally follow up with ways to be helpful.

In order to properly network, it is imperative that you utilize all of the steps of networking. You cannot build a team without people, but you want to find quality people so you can have a quality team. **Network where you want to go not where you are. Your network determines your net-worth.**

If you want to be a teacher, then network with teachers that have influence and experience. If you want to be a successful entrepreneur then network with entrepreneurs that are successful and are willing to teach. Networking is an essential action to take in order to begin building your team.

Furthermore, the art of persuasion and influence are the bedrock of recruiting and retaining. You cannot win the game of life without a team around you. Now that we know how to properly network with people, we must now cover giving them what they want.

The first question one should ask when presented with this action is: *What do the people want?*

If you can tap into one or more things that are at the core of every human's desires, you can build a team and you can win. People want four fundamental things for a fulfilled life: they want benefits, family, fun, and hope.

Benefits are simply front end value and back end value. Whenever someone is looking for a job, the ideal job has good 'benefits.' The money that somebody makes from their job is the front end value, and the insurance, retirement options, vacation perks, and sick time are the back end value.

As a leader looking to build a winning team you must clearly articulate the front and back end value that a person will gain from joining your team. The benefits you identify should help solve problems in someone's life. In order to get the right people on your team you have to be able to clearly articulate what the benefits of being on your team are. Is it money? Is it a t-shirt? Is it status? Is it something sentimental or priceless?

Be able to clearly tell someone how their life will be better or what problem you will solve in their life once they become a part of your team.

The next thing people want is family. I reiterate **relatives are the people that have your name, family are the people that have your back**. You have to learn how to make people feel like your family.

Family helps people feel comfort and significance. We mentioned earlier that everyone desires to be significant. Family helps, listens, and appreciates their own. People want to be helped, they want to be heard, they want to be liked, appreciated, and they want to matter. If you can show people that they are liked, they are appreciated, and that they matter, you will have their allegiance in whatever you want to do. They will be on your team and they will not leave.

People also want to have fun. If you are the manager of an office, planning an event, or the leader of a family with small children, you have to have fun. Fun can be integrated into anything, make sure there is always an element of fun within the work you do. Add a wacky t-shirt day to the office calendar. Good clean fun is always appreciated and welcomed. Nobody likes a leader that cannot laugh at life. So when you are building your team be sure to integrate fun into what you do.

Lastly, the people want hope. They want a better tomorrow. Make sure you take the right actions to show them that their life will be better because of their interaction with you. Don't tell them, take action and show them that they have hope. A great way to instill hope in others is to constantly show them things to be grateful for. If you can be grateful, you can believe in a brighter future.

Building a team is only important because none of us will be here forever. How do you know that an orange tree is an orange tree if you've never seen one before? It would be easier if there were oranges on the tree. The greatest and most famous person that I believe ever lived was The Messiah, The Christ. There was a story in the Bible where He was walking along the road and identified a fig tree.

Apparently, in the story he was hungry because once he discovered the fig tree did not have any figs he condemned it. He cursed the tree and said that it should not ever produce figs again. It immediately withered and died. I guess His thought process was, since the fig tree was not bearing fruit for Him to eat then it is no good and should not ever bear fruit. My hope is to never be cursed and condemned like the tree was. In order to avoid that we all need to bear fruit. If you fail to bear fruit then you will not win in anything. **Only what you do for others will last. What you do for others is your fruit.**

Bearing fruit is all about reproducing success. A wise man once said **you cannot be truly successful until you produce a successor**. In other words, you cannot truly be successful until you have someone come after you to continue your success.

Bearing fruit means you leave a legacy of excellence. It takes a team to leave a legacy. You will win by making it easier for others to win as well. You make it easier for others to win by doing these three things: (1) Study, (2) Live, and (3) Teach.

Success leaves footprints, so follow them. Study how you want to live and teach what you live. Whatever industry you are a part of; study those that have been successful in it. Then after your study, live what you have studied. You study to live and you teach how you live. Once you do that you will perpetuate success.

Others will come behind you and do what you did to become successful. Though you may or may not directly affect the lives of some, **the way you live speaks louder than anything you will ever say.** Becoming a better leader is all about making others around you the best that they can be. Take action today.

Game Plan Review

- Wake up with a sense of urgency. Be aware, be alert, and prioritize your life.

- Build a team. Network. Make sure the people that become a part of your network understand the benefits of being in the network, are treated like family, have fun, and are given hope.

- Bear fruit, reproduce successful people.

- Study. Live. Teach.

CHAPTER 7

Courage

I'd rather have a life full of oh wells, than a life full of what ifs.

The 'C' in IMPACT stands for courage. In order to win the game of life you must be courageous. Courage is defined as many things by different people, but I want to pull a quote yet again from Mark Twain to establish a foundation of what courage is in this chapter.

Years ago, Twain said, **twenty years from now you will be more disappointed by the things that you didn't do than by the ones you did do. So throw off the bowlines. Sail away from the safe harbor. Catch the trade winds in your sails. Explore. Dream.**

Discover. Most people spend their lives either being incredibly conservative or haphazardly ambitious.

My advice to you is to be conservatively ambitious. Early in my life I was haphazardly ambitious. I would take on ventures and do business deals just based on the money I could potentially make. I did not take the time to do the proper due diligence, in other words I under analyzed.

You need to have the courage to move forward intelligently to succeed. This is why it is important to define what winning is in your life. The things that I did early in my business life were based on the notion that I wanted to get rich quick without doing much work. Getting rich quick is not a bad thing necessarily, it is the idea of getting rich without a ton of blood, sweat and tears that is bad. **Winning in life is not easy**. I hope that since you have read this far you understand that.

Life can present very formidable opposition. You cannot fold due to fear. As the saying goes, **fear will kill more dreams than failure ever will**. It's okay to be afraid as long as you don't let fear freeze you. It is okay to be afraid, as long as you are still effective in the game. Some people use the statement, life is not fair, to account for the losses in their life. Perhaps someone told those people that upon entry into this world we were supposed to be given a level playing field. This is untrue. **Life is not supposed to be fair, life is supposed to be conquered. Life is supposed to be mastered.**

The game of life will not consider our complaints as a sign to let up. **Life does not want our complaints, life wants our competition.** We are placed in the positions we are in not to cripple us, but to qualify us. So if you were born in a single parent household, in the projects, or with a disability of some sort you have a great obstacle. Whatever your obstacle is it was given to you to strengthen you not strangle you. Also consider every time you desire to move up to another level there will be a bigger obstacle to qualify you. Take courage. Do not be afraid. Embrace the challenge and win anyway.

As we analyze the overall call to take courage, I want to inform you that we must have different types of courage in order to win the game of life. There are four types of courage we will discuss in this chapter. They are: (1) The courage to fail, (2) The courage to speak confidently in front of others, (3) The courage to have integrity, and (4) The courage to sacrifice.

Be Persistent & Consistent

Let me preface the details of the different types of courage by explaining that they should all be accompanied with persistence and consistence.

Persistence and consistence are alike, but they are not the same. If you are consistent, that means you have made a habit of doing something. For example, undoubtedly everyone reading these words brushes their teeth after they wake up in the morning. You are indeed consistent in brushing your teeth because you do this action repeatedly. That is consistence.

Persistence is when you persevere in the midst of obstacles. In other words in one aspect of life you overcame something. Persistence in the tooth brushing analogy would be if you overcame getting up late or not having toothpaste to still successfully brush your teeth.

You can be persistent without being consistent. There are individuals that have been persistent in one area of life, or at one time in their life, but not in any other areas, or not in more than one instance. When stepping into the winners' circle of life, you must be persistent *and* consistent. Life happens to us every day, and every day we must be consistent in overcoming the challenges we will face. We must resolve to be consistently and persistently courageous.

The Courage to Fail

The one who fails the most often and the most intelligently will eventually become the most

successful. If you see someone that is successful, then you have seen someone who has been pierced with the sharp edge of failure multiple times. They just continued to move forward despite the failure they experienced. Winston Churchill offered an amazing quote for continuous effort, **continuous effort, not strength or intelligence, is the key to unlocking our potential. Success is not final, failure is not fatal, it is the courage to continue that counts.**

To have courage you must have faith. If you don't have faith, then you need no courage. Fear and faith occupy the same space in your mind, but there is only room for one or the other. There will be times that things will be scary, but your faith appears to dissipate your fear. John Wayne had a special way of defining courage, **courage is being scared to death, and saddling up anyway.**

Courage is the ability to disregard fear and act anyway. The Latin root of the word courage is cur, which means heart. Courage literally means to "take heart." Fear exists along a continuum. Courage involves recognizing a reasonable amount of fear or nervousness, facing it and then taking an intelligent risk. Note the word *intelligent* in the previous sentence. Don't be foolish in taking risks, be shrewd.

A few years before this book was released, Will Smith

and his son Jaden Smith starred in a movie entitled *After Earth*. There is a dynamic saying in that movie that headlined all of the advertising up through the time the film came out. Will Smith's character in the movie said that: **Danger is very real, but fear is a choice.** Things can be scary and difficult to face, but at this point in your life you have to make the choice to look danger (failure) in the eye and say: Give me your best shot!

In order to truly decide whether or not you should be operating with courage in a particular area, you have to assess your reason for being brave. This leads me back to the point of taking intelligent risks. Sometimes people courageously do things that do not take them closer to their goals. In the iconic movie trilogy *Back to the Future* the antagonist Biff Tannen would often get the protagonist Marty McFly (played by Michael J. Fox) to make a bad mistake by causing him to misplace his courage.

His famous line was always: "What are you chicken McFly?" Then Marty would respond by saying, "Nobody calls me chicken!" Marty would then play right into Biff's hands and fall right into a trap that would almost leave him destroyed. In any regard, Marty never wanted to appear afraid, so when Biff would call him a name, he would courageously face him, but it took him further away from his goal.

Be sure that you are intelligently courageous. If you want to jump out of a plane, make sure you have a parachute and you know how to use it. Have the courage to fail when the potential to win takes you closer to achieving something worthwhile. Know your goal and make sure your activity moves you towards it and not further away.

Speak Confidently

No matter the industry or the market, those that have the confidence to speak in front of other people will be of high value. Before I began professionally speaking, I heard the saying that public speaking was among people's top fears. You can make the choice to conquer that fear or let it conquer you. Speaking in front of others either in a small group setting, an interview setting, or a large group setting is a skill you have to acquire but that skill can only be acquired if you are willing to learn.

Your ability to be eloquent, confident, and clear when you speak is critically important. The best way to learn this skill is to join a group like Toastmasters and fully participate. You don't have to become a professional motivational speaker or anything of that nature, but you should be able to comfortably and confidently share what is in your mind. Do not believe the myth that being able to speak clearly and confidently is an innate skill. You can learn to do it, you just have to have the courage to learn how to do it.

People that earn the most money and hold top positions in their companies and organizations all have attained this skill. Words are powerful and they have the ability to change the course of one's life. Be a wise distributor of words in front of people that matter, as it relates to reaching your goals. A great way to develop confidence is to be knowledgeable about your subject matter. If you know the topic well, then it is easier to speak confidently in front of other people.

Another reason why you should have the courage to speak confidently in front of other people is simply because some people will never speak up for themselves. A lot of people operate in fear to speak up for themselves, for an idea they have, or for a problem others have. This is one way speaking confidently helps you win the game of life. Being an articulate mouthpiece for individuals and groups that do not have a voice can help start movements, raise money, and shine light on things that are dwelling in the darkness. You can do it, and I believe you will.

Have Integrity

To piggyback on the saying used by Will Smith in the movie *After Earth*, I will say not only is danger very real, but so is evil. Evil is the absence of good. Evil is the foundation of the word devil, and I shouldn't have to emphasize how important that is. I believe if you are reading this, you know the difference between what is right and what is wrong. I will spare giving you a list of rights and wrongs (see the law for that). There are times, however, when doing the right thing is not easy.

There are times when it is easier and more beneficial to tell a lie, but it is not the right thing to do. In dealings with your family, friends, your co-workers, and your colleagues, have the courage to have integrity. Have the courage to be honest and operate with morals.

If you consistently operate in continual deceit, illegal activity, and dishonesty, it will catch up with you. I often think about some of my favorite athletes who lost the fortunes and much of the fame they had because of a lack of integrity. Working in a jail for five years showed me firsthand that decent and very normal people can succumb to the dark side of the law.

If you are consistently honest with people they will trust and respect you a great deal. Honesty and fairness are high commodities in a society of greed and selfishness. **Have the courage to do what's right in a world that will celebrate you if you do the right kind of wrong.** Being a person of integrity is all about understanding the long term benefits of doing right. I want to repeat the saying written earlier found in the most famous book ever written that says, **for what does it profit a man to gain the whole world, but lose his soul?**

That saying was quoted by the greatest and most famous man that ever lived. I believe He said this to emphasize that life is much more than what we see. If someone were to gain the whole world, they would have everything that we could see. They would have all the money, cars, houses, and other material things that people would want. Integrity does not always mean that you do the right thing every time. Integrity means that when you know that no one is looking, you still resolve to do the right thing. Oprah Winfrey puts it like this, **real integrity is doing the right thing knowing that nobody's going to know whether you did it or not.**

Gaining the entire world may seem like a good deal, especially since your soul is an unseen thing. What does a soul look like? I am not sure that anyone knows, but the lesson here is that what is seen is temporary and what is unseen is not. In the face of adversity be consistent and persistent in having integrity. Thomas Paine asserted that, **reputation is what men and** women think of us; character is what God and angels know of us.

Sacrifice

Sacrifice is the ability to give up something you like for something that you love. Sometimes making a sacrifice is hard. At times you have to give up a relationship with someone. Other times you may have to work a job you don't want to work to better position yourself for something greater in the future. Dr. Dennis Kimbro said it like this, **if you will live 2 years like your friends won't, you can live the rest of your life like your friends can't.**

I love that quote, but there are two types of sacrifices presented within it. The first sacrifice is to live differently. This entire book has been about how to win the game of life. Indicated within the metaphor of the game of life is doing 'life' differently than others. You may have to listen to different music than your friends. You may have to watch different shows, read different books, visit different places, and adopt different habits.

Upon living differently than your friends for a small amount of time (2 years), you can live the rest of your life like they will not be able to. **It should be your goal to be the most disciplined person that you know.** Get more done. Be more consistent. Beat down the door to your dreams and goals with persistence. Win. **Sacrifice by living differently.**

The other sacrifice mentioned in the quote above is hidden between the lines. If you consistently live differently than your friends then more than likely they will no longer be your friends. In other words, you must be willing to sacrifice certain relationships. For many people, this may be a difficult or unthinkable thing. It is something that all people must eventually do. Usually people are linked in friendships through proximity and commonalities.

If you share the same values and live close to your friends, more than likely you will stay connected to them. When one of those elements is deleted from the equation, your friendship will dissipate or not be as intimate. Sometimes winning the game of life means that you have to disassociate or limit your association with certain people.

Consistently employing courage in your life along with the persistence to overcome the enemies of your courage will allow you to win in life. It's okay to be afraid, but it is not okay to do nothing in the face of fear. **Winners fail until they quit, losers quit when they fail.** Winners act in spite of fear and move toward their goals in life. Take heart, look in the face of fear and win anyway.

Game Plan Review

- Be persistent and consistent in battling the enemies of your courage.

- Understand that danger and evil are real, but have the courage to overcome each when necessary.

- Have the courage to fail when facing worthy goals.

- Have the courage to speak confidently in front of others.

- Have the courage to have integrity. Do the right thing when no one is watching.

- Have the courage to sacrifice for the greater good.

CHAPTER 8

Transformation

In the museum of life be the artist that paints a vivid picture of a better tomorrow.

The last letter in the word IMPACT is 'T' which stands for Transformation. It fittingly ties a nice neat bow on the *Refuse to Lose* game plan. Winners are transformed. Being transformed means that you are consistently becoming what you are destined to be. Once you are transformed, you will have a clear vision of a better tomorrow. You will not only see the possibilities of tomorrow, but you take the possibilities of tomorrow and live in them. If you've ever played on a sports team, then you have undoubtedly seen the results of transformation. At the beginning of the season, the team is very different than at the end of the season (hopefully for the better).

Transformation holds true in relationships. During the dating phase things feel different than they do after being with the same person 5 years later. The key to a successful transformation is knowing what you want to transform into and taking the necessary steps to do it.

Our tomorrow is a combination of what we do today and what we did yesterday. How do you truly win? You win by creating a better tomorrow today, and teaching those that you serve to do the same. In other words, you have to cast a vision for yourself, and teach others to do the same.

Transformation Comes from Vision

Regular people have sight, winners have vision. **Sight is viewed with eyes, vision is seen with faith.** Faith is the substance of things hoped for and the evidence of things not seen. In order to have a great vision, you must believe that things will be better than they currently are. Helen Keller said **the most pathetic person in the world is someone who has sight, but has no vision.** Put another way, without vision you do not transform, you remain the same.

Vision centers on having goals. This connects back to what was stated in the beginning of the book, you have to decide what 'winning' looks like. There are good transformations and there are bad transformations. Good transformations only happen with a clear vision and a subsequent action plan. Bad transformations happen when you do nothing. Most people can gain weight with no thought or vision. On the other hand losing weight and maintaining a healthy lifestyle has to include a vision with multiple goals. Make a goal to transform into something greater every single day.

Make a goal to set records in your company or organization. Raise the most money in a non-profit venture in your area. Goals are simply dreams with a deadline. When I left my job all I had were goals. I wanted to book 20 speaking dates in about a 4-5 month span. I did that and more. I'm not telling you that to impress you. I tell you that because for you to have a better tomorrow, you have to have faith to see it before it comes. Accompanied with that faith are the works to make it a reality. Inaction nullifies faith.

Not only is the practice of goal setting key in your transformation and necessary for creating a better tomorrow, but it is essential to pass on to those you serve. Aristotle famously said **excellence is never an accident. It is always the result of high intention, sincere effort, and intelligent execution; it represents the wise choice of many alternatives - choice, not chance, and determines your destiny.**

Give the people you serve a reason to become excellent. Teach them to set goals that will make them worthy of becoming a winner in their own right. Worthy goals are goals that make something of you when you achieve them. If you set a goal to make a million dollars, the prize really isn't the million dollars. The prize is what you transform into on the way to obtaining the million. Your ultimate goal to win will transform you into a winner.

Remember the four areas of life I mentioned earlier that we should all win in: Faith, Family, Fitness, and Finances. Be sure to have a worthy goal attached to these areas. If you neglect any one of these four areas, then what you transform into may not be ideal. However, do not fail to help others do the same. Helping others develop powerful questions to advance their lives should be something you resolve to do. Help others see a brighter tomorrow by showing them their faith through their goals.

Another component of vision comes from having a mission. Goals will build the foundation for your mission, but there is more to a mission than what you accomplish. After you achieve all of your goals and transform into the person you are destined to become, how is it connected to the greater good?

Connecting your purpose to a specific mission is

critical to transformation. People become successful without having a mission, but they usually do not win. Winning involves others. Transformation involves others. Other people have to see the fruit of what we have done. Sustained success is the result of a mission and a vision. Make sure that your mission helps other people. What is beautiful about the universe is that you can be intelligently self-interested and still make a positive change.

Former President Woodrow Wilson said you are not here merely to make a living. He eloquently stated **you are here in order to enable the world to live more amply, with greater vision, with a finer spirit of hope and achievement. You are here to enrich the world, and you impoverish yourself if you forget the errand.**

I hope you understood that quote. Playing small does not help anybody or anything, not even your fears. Being connected to a mission enhances your vision and assigns a purpose to your everyday activities.

A FINAL WORD

efuse to Lose may sound like a cliché rallying call by a losing team's coach that may produce an epic comeback. It may even seem like a cheesy motivational tape someone may have made millions of dollars on in the 1950s selling Amway. Above all of these things, it is a call to transform people into winners. We all need different mnemonic devices to remember why we want to succeed. In my experience, thinking about life as a sport or a game helps because it makes things easier to measure. **There can be no forward movement without keen measurement.**

As you look at your notes and your highlights from this book, I want to leave you with a final word when considering the information presented before you. **Choose this day how you will win and simply, win.** If you are a college student that defines winning as a college degree with a 4.0 GPA, then win. If you are an entrepreneur who defines winning as making a six figure income after taxes, then win. If you are a married couple that defines winning as getting out of debt, then win. Whatever winning is to you, refuse to lose, and win. The distractions of the day can easily derail us from our destinies.

You may very well get distracted by an event, that's when you need to tell yourself: "I REFUSE TO LOSE!" That's when you must tell yourself, I may not have won yesterday, but today my victory will make up for all of the previous days I have lost. Attack the enemy of your victory. Review the game plan that has been laid out before you. It has worked for countless others including myself. **Don't make excuses, make progress.** Don't accept failure, but rather take victory! I cannot wait to hear your story someday, maybe we can write it together. Cheers to your victory!

Odell Bizzell is a blogger, author, internet personality, and dynamic keynote speaker. While in high school Odell started a small candy retail distribution center that earned him over $75,000 while earning an academic scholarship to college. Odell has been featured in the USA Today, Yahoo Finance, CNBC.com, and over 200 media outlets. He's also the author of 4 books and is a nationally recognized expert in perseverance training and leadership. Odell has presented on the same stages as Super Bowl winning coaches, Senior Political Advisor for the Obama administration Dave Axelrod, Dave Letterman, & Oprah Winfrey.

To book Odell for your next speaking event, stay abreast of his experiences, and connect to him visit:

www.OdellBizzell.com

Made in the USA
Middletown, DE
17 July 2019